by Susan Wood
illustrated by Burgandy Beam

Editorial Offices: Glenview, Illinois • Parsippany, New Jersey • New York, New York
Sales Offices: Needham, Massachusetts • Duluth, Georgia • Glenview, Illinois
Coppell, Texas • Ontario, California • Mesa, Arizona

Every effort has been made to secure permission and provide appropriate credit for photographic material. The publisher deeply regrets any omission and pledges to correct errors called to its attention in subsequent editions.

Unless otherwise acknowledged, all photographs are the property of Scott Foresman, a division of Pearson Education.

Illustrations by Burgandy Beam

ISBN: 0-328-13421-X

Copyright © Pearson Education, Inc.

All Rights Reserved. Printed in the United States of America. This publication is protected by Copyright, and permission should be obtained from the publisher prior to any prohibited reproduction, storage in a retrieval system, or transmission in any form by any means, electronic, mechanical, photocopying, recording, or likewise. For information regarding permission(s), write to: Permissions Department, Scott Foresman, 1900 East Lake Avenue, Glenview, Illinois 60025.

8 9 10 V0G1 14 13 12 11 10 09 08

Jimmy and his parents finished loading their family camper. It was time to leave for their annual camping trip in western North Dakota. Jimmy loved riding in the family camper across the wide, open prairie. He could not wait to use the new sleeping bag he received for his birthday. Jimmy's dad drove while his mom took a nap in the front seat.

Jimmy stared out the window. He watched ranchers as they lassoed runaway cattle in the prairie grasses. He pictured himself on a galloping horse and began daydreaming about life on a ranch. Jimmy paid no attention to the dark clouds that were rolling in fast.

Then Jimmy heard a crash of thunder and he jumped.

He looked up front to see his mom wide awake. His dad was watching the road carefully through the rain.

Jimmy felt his body grow tense. He hated thunder and lightning. The loud noises always scared him. His mom looked back at him. She smiled, reached back, and patted his knee.

"Don't worry, it's just a little rain," Jimmy's dad said. "We're safe as long as the river does not overflow its riverbed."

"That's right," said Jimmy's mom. "I need you to do two favors for me. Try not to be scared, honey, and help me keep an eye on the water. Let me know if it looks like it's getting higher."

"OK," said Jimmy, trying to be brave. He turned and looked back out the window.

Jimmy's mom flipped on the radio in the camper. "We need to listen to the weather report," she said.

A voice on the radio was talking about the danger of flash floods. Jimmy's parents quickly glanced at each other. They looked worried.

Jimmy kept watching the river. The whipping wind shrieked outside the camper. Jimmy felt more and more nervous.

"The dry ground of these riverbeds can become almost as hard as rocks. When it rains, the hardened riverbed cannot absorb all the water," the radio announcer said. "Riverbeds can overflow during rain storms, flooding roads and houses. It happens really fast. That's why they are called flash floods. Drivers beware: In a flood, it takes only two feet of water to wash away a car."

Jimmy pictured rushing water overflowing a dry riverbed as he stared out the window.

Soon what Jimmy was seeing was not his imagination.

"Mom! The river is overflowing!" he yelled.

"OK, Jimmy. Now we need to be quiet so your father can drive," she said. "The water is still pretty far from the road."

But Jimmy felt scared. The water was inching closer to the edge of the road. He was sure they would get washed away.

Jimmy's dad drove the camper around a bend. His mom craned her neck to get a better view.

"Looks like the road is flooded up ahead," said Jimmy's mom.

"We'd better not drive through that water," decided Jimmy's dad. "We should head for higher ground."

Jimmy gulped. His dad parked the camper on the high side of the road. They all got out.

"OK," Jimmy's dad said, "We're going to have to leave the camper here."

Jimmy seemed offended by the idea. "But what about my new sleeping bag?" he asked.

"I'll make a bargain with you," Jimmy's dad said. He quickly handed Jimmy a jar of peanut butter and a bag with bread and plastic silverware. "If you carry these things for me right now, I'll buy you new camping gear later. We have to get moving right now."

Jimmy felt sick. His stomach was in a knot. He worried about the camper. He worried about himself and his parents. He did what his dad told him to do.

His mother grabbed a bottle of water from the camper. His father locked the doors. They quickly started to walk away from the camper.

Jimmy and his family hurried away from the road and up a hill. Climbing made them tired and wet. "My legs hurt," said Jimmy.

"I know this is hard," said Jimmy's dad. "But we still need to climb higher. We'll be safest up there."

Together they climbed the hill and hoped the storm would pass.

It was a long hike to the top. The road was flooded when the family made it to safety. As the rain let up, the family ate some sandwiches. Jimmy's dad took out his cellular phone.

"Who are you calling, Dad?" Jimmy asked.

"The state police," he said. "I want to tell them about the road and let them know we are OK in case they find our camper."

Finally, the storm passed. Jimmy's family hiked back to the camper. Luckily, it had not been washed away in the flood. Their belongings were safe.

There was a state trooper waiting by the camper. He said, "You folks were really smart. It was a good idea to head for higher ground. We had almost ten inches of rain in just a couple of hours."

During the rest of the vacation Jimmy kept watching for storms. On the prairie you never know when a flash flood might hit.

What to Do During a Flash Flood

- Know how to get away from low areas. Look for hills to climb to safety.
- Keep bottled water and enough food to last a few days.
- Have a first-aid kit nearby.
- Listen to weather updates.
- Do not try to outrun a flood.
- Do not try to walk or swim through flood waters. A person can be swept away by only six inches of water.

Rain falls to the Earth from clouds. After a storm, the ground absorbs some rain water. Some runs off into rivers, lakes, and oceans. Some turns into vapor, or steam, when it is heated by the sun. The vapor goes into the air and collects to form clouds so it can rain again. Flash floods happen when there is more rain than the ground or watersheds can handle.